Database Administrator Guide

Practical Guide

A. De Quattro

Database Administrator Guide

Introduction

A Database Administrator (DBA) plays a pivotal role in managing, maintaining, and securing databases to ensure that data is stored, retrieved, and maintained efficiently and effectively. In today's data-driven world, the DBA is critical to the operational success of any organization that relies on a database to store and manage its data. This role encompasses a range of responsibilities, from performance tuning and disaster recovery to security management and architecture design.

Chapter 1: Fundamentals of Databases

What are Databases?

A database is an organized collection of structured information, or data, typically stored electronically in a computer system. Databases are managed by Database Management Systems (DBMS), which provide a systematic way to create, retrieve, update, and manage data. DBMS help users and other applications interact with the data. The data in a database can be stored in various formats and can be accessed through various interfaces, including command line tools, graphical user interfaces, and web applications.

Databases can range in size from a few megabytes to several terabytes, encompassing data about a wide variety of subjects. They are utilized in a multitude of applications, including enterprise systems, web applications, and personal applications. Examples of popular DBMS include Oracle, Microsoft SQL Server, MySQL, PostgreSQL, and MongoDB.

Types of Databases

Databases can be categorized into several types based on their structure and use cases. The most common types include relational databases, non-relational databases, and NoSQL databases.

Relational Databases

Relational databases are the most prevalent type of database. They store data in tables, which consist of rows and columns. Each row in a table represents a single record, while each column represents an attribute of that record. Relational databases use Structured Query Language (SQL) for defining and manipulating data.

Key characteristics of relational databases include:

- **Data Integrity:** Relational databases enforce data integrity through primary keys, foreign keys, and constraints.

- **ACID Compliance:** Transactions in relational databases adhere to the ACID properties (Atomicity, Consistency, Isolation, Durability), which ensure reliable processing of database transactions.

- **Schema:** Relational databases use a predefined schema, which requires a structured approach to data design.

Popular relational databases include MySQL, PostgreSQL, Microsoft SQL Server, and Oracle Database.

Non-Relational Databases

In contrast to relational databases, non-relational databases, or "NoSQL" databases, do not rely on a fixed schema or structured tables. They are designed to handle large volumes of unstructured and semi-structured data, providing more flexibility in data modeling and storage.

Key characteristics of non-relational databases include:

- **Scalability:** Non-relational databases can easily scale horizontally by adding more servers.

- **Flexibility:** They allow the storage of diverse data types and structures without requiring a predefined schema.

Common types of non-relational databases

include:

- **Document Stores:** Such as MongoDB and CouchDB, which store data in JSON-like documents.

- **Key-Value Stores:** Such as Redis and Amazon DynamoDB, which store data as key-value pairs.

- **Column-Family Stores:** Such as Apache Cassandra and HBase, which store data in columns instead of rows, making them efficient for analytical queries.

- **Graph Databases:** Such as Neo4j and Amazon Neptune, which are optimized for traversing relationships between data.

NoSQL Databases

NoSQL is a specific category of non-relational databases that provides a wide array of data models designed to fit varying organizational requirements. Unlike traditional relational databases, NoSQL databases are geared for high-volume data storage, retrieval, and performance, making them suitable for big data applications and real-time web applications.

NoSQL databases typically fall into four categories:

1. **Document Databases:** They allow data to be stored in document format, making them perfect for content management systems, blog platforms, and e-commerce applications.

2. **Key-Value Stores:** These offer a simple data storage model with a key-value architecture, suitable for caching, user sessions, and other high-traffic applications.

3. **Wide-Column Stores:** They provide complex data structures suitable for analytical

queries and allow for a lot of flexibility in how data is queried.

4. **Graph Databases:** This type connects nodes and edges for efficient data traversal, perfect for social networks, recommendation engines, and fraud detection systems.

Relational Model and Alternative Models

The relational model, proposed by Edgar F. Codd in the 1970s, revolutionized how data is structured and accessed in databases. In the relational model, data is represented as a collection of relations (or tables), where each relation consists of tuples (rows) and attributes (columns). The relationships among data entities are established through foreign keys, which link two tables together.

Alternatives to the relational model include various non-relational models such as:

- **Document Model:** Focuses on storing, retrieving, and managing document-oriented information like JSON or XML.

- **Key-Value Model:** Simple option to store data as key-value pairs, making it fast and efficient for certain types of applications.

- **Column-Family Model:** Optimized for analytical processing, where data is organized into columns.

- **Graph Model:** Allows complex relationships and connections among data points, facilitating deep link traversals.

Each model has its strengths and considerations, and the choice depends largely on the specific needs of the application being developed.

Normalization and Denormalization

Normalization is a database design technique aimed at organizing data to reduce redundancy and improve data integrity. The normalization process involves dividing large tables into smaller, related tables and defining relationships between them. Normalization is achieved through a series of "normal forms," which provide a framework for achieving higher levels of data organization.

Key benefits of normalization include:

- **Reduced Redundancy:** Minimizing duplicate data entries saves storage space and reduces the risk of inconsistent data.

- **Data Integrity:** Ensuring data dependencies are properly enforced.

However, there are also trade-offs, such as:

- **Complexity:** More tables may increase the complexity of queries and require more joins.

- **Performance Impact:** Joins can slow down query performance, especially in large databases.

In some scenarios, denormalization—a process that involves combining multiple tables into fewer ones—may be a favorable approach. Denormalization can reduce the number of joins required in queries, which can improve performance, particularly in read-heavy applications. However, it introduces the risk of data redundancy and potential integrity issues.

As organizations navigate the complexities of data management, the role of a Database Administrator has become increasingly vital. This chapter introduced fundamental concepts related to databases, including what they are, the types of databases available, the relational model versus alternatives, and normalization and denormalization. Understanding these foundational elements is essential for any aspiring DBA or data professional. In the following chapters, we will delve deeper into specific roles and responsibilities of a DBA, best practices for database management, and emerging trends in the field.

Chapter 2: Database Management Systems (DBMS)

Introduction to DBMS

Database Management Systems (DBMS) are software systems that enable users to define, create, maintain, and control access to databases. They serve as intermediaries between users and the databases they manage, ensuring that data is stored, retrieved, and manipulated efficiently and securely. DBMSs play a crucial role in handling large amounts of data, enforcing data integrity, and providing tools for backup and recovery.

The primary responsibilities of a DBMS include data storage, data retrieval, data manipulation, and data administration. DBMSs can handle a variety of data types including structured data (e.g., relational databases) and unstructured data (e.g., NoSQL databases). The increasing volume of data generated in today's digital age necessitates efficient and robust database solutions, leading to a surge in the use of DBMS technologies.

Key Functions of a DBMS

1. **Data Definition**: DBMS allows users to define the structure of the data to be stored, including data types, formats, and relationships. This is often accomplished using Data Definition Language (DDL).

2. **Data Manipulation**: Users can create, read, update, and delete (CRUD) data using Data Manipulation Language (DML). DBMS provides a systematic approach to managing these operations.

3. **Data Security**: A DBMS enforces security mechanisms to protect stored data, ensuring that only authorized users can access

or manipulate data.

4. **Data Integrity**: DBMS maintains data integrity through constraints and validation rules that prevent the entry of incorrect or inconsistent data.

5. **Backup and Recovery**: A DBMS provides tools for data backup and recovery in the event of data loss or corruption, ensuring that data is recoverable.

6. **Concurrency Control**: A DBMS manages multiple users accessing the database simultaneously, providing mechanisms that prevent conflicts and maintain data consistency.

7. **Data Abstraction**: DBMS abstracts the complexities of data storage from users, providing an easier interface to interact with the database.

In summary, a DBMS simplifies the management of data, improves efficiency, enforces security measures, and ensures that data remains consistent and reliable.

Overview of Major DBMS

1. MySQL

MySQL is one of the most popular open-source relational database management systems. It is widely used for web applications and is known for its reliability and performance. Users can execute SQL queries, which makes it suitable for both beginners and experienced developers. MySQL provides features such as replication, partitioning, and a robust set of storage engines.

Key Features:

- **Open Source**: Free to use and has a

large community for support.

- **Cross-Platform**: Available on multiple operating systems.

- **ACID Compliance**: Supports transactions that ensure data integrity.

- **Scalability**: Suitable for small to large database applications.

2. PostgreSQL

PostgreSQL is an advanced, open-source object-relational database system. It is known for its robustness and feature set that includes complex queries and foreign key constraints. PostgreSQL supports a wide variety of data types and offers extensibility with custom functions, operators, and more.

Key Features:

- **Extensible**: Users can create their own data types and functions.

- **Standards Compliance**: Conforms closely to SQL standards.

- **Concurrency Control**: Uses Multi-Version Concurrency Control (MVCC).

- **Geospatial Capabilities**: Offers powerful geographic data types and functions.

3. Oracle Database

Oracle Database is a comprehensive, enterprise-grade database management system produced by Oracle Corporation. It offers extensive features tailored for large businesses, including automatic storage management, data security, and complex analytics capabilities.

Key Features:

- **High Performance**: Optimized for high transactions and large databases.

- **Advanced Security**: Features like data

encryption and user management.

- **Multitenant Architecture**: Supports multiple databases in a consolidated manner.

- **Data Warehousing and Analytics**: Built-in data analysis tools.

4. Microsoft SQL Server

Microsoft SQL Server is a relational database management system developed by Microsoft. It is designed for enterprise environments and provides a wide range of tools and solutions for managing, analyzing, and reporting on data.

Key Features:

- **Integration with Microsoft Tools**: Seamless connectivity with other Microsoft products like Excel and Power BI.

- **Data Analysis Capabilities**: Built-in analytics tools and reporting services.

- **High Availability**: Features like Always On availability groups.

- **Security**: Advanced security features including dynamic data masking.

5. MongoDB

MongoDB is a popular NoSQL database that is document-oriented. It is designed to store unstructured data and is known for its high scalability and flexibility. MongoDB uses JSON-like documents that allow for faster and more efficient data retrieval.

Key Features:

- **Schema-less**: Supports unstructured and semi-structured data.

- **Horizontal Scalability**: Can easily scale out by adding more servers.

- **Rich Query Language**: Supports complex queries and indexing.

- **Aggregation Framework**: Provides powerful data processing capabilities.

Installation and Configuration of a DBMS

Setting up a DBMS typically involves a series of steps that include downloading the software, installing it, and configuring the necessary settings for optimal performance.

MySQL Installation Steps

1. **Download**: Go to the official MySQL website and download the installation package for your operating system.

2. **Run Installer**: Execute the installer and follow the on-screen instructions. Choose the installation type (Developer, Server, etc.).

3. **Configure MySQL Server**: During installation, you'll be prompted to configure the server settings including setting a root password and choosing server configuration options.

4. **Start MySQL**: After configuration, start the MySQL server service either from the terminal or using a service manager specific to your OS.

5. **Access MySQL**: Use a MySQL client or command line to connect to the server using your credentials.

PostgreSQL Installation Steps

1. **Download**: Visit the PostgreSQL official website and select the version suitable for your OS.

2. **Run Installer**: Execute the downloaded installer, and during installation, specify the installation directory and data directory.

3. **User Setup**: Configure the superuser account (usually the 'postgres' user) and set the password.

4. **Configure Service**: Enable the PostgreSQL service to start automatically upon system startup.

5. **Client Access**: You can access the database via command line (psql) or graphical tools like pgAdmin.

Oracle Database Installation Steps

1. **Download**: Access the Oracle Technology Network and download the Oracle Database installation files.

2. **Run Installer**: Execute the Oracle Universal Installer, and follow the prompts to install and configure the database.

3. **Create Database**: During installation, choose to create a database and specify the database name and configuration options.

4. **Setup Environment Variables**: Configure environment variables (e.g., ORACLE_HOME) to facilitate database access.

5. **Access the Database**: Use SQL*Plus or Oracle SQL Developer to connect to the database.

Microsoft SQL Server Installation Steps

1. **Download**: Go to the Microsoft website and download the SQL Server

installation package.

2. **Run Installer**: Launch the installer and choose the installation type (New SQL Server stand-alone installation).

3. **Select Features**: Choose the features to install (e.g., Database Engine, Analysis Services).

4. **Configuration**: Configure server settings including authentication mode, SQL Server administrator accounts, and others.

5. **Complete Installation**: Finish the installation and access SQL Server via SQL Server Management Studio (SSMS).

MongoDB Installation Steps

1. **Download**: Download the MongoDB Community Server from the official MongoDB website.

2. **Run Installer**: Execute the installer selecting the necessary options.

3. **Configure MongoDB**: Optionally, create a configuration file for MongoDB settings or run it with default settings.

4. **Start Service**: Launch the MongoDB service using command line or system service manager.

5. **Client Access**: Use the MongoDB Shell (mongosh) for database operations.

Interacting with a DBMS via GUI and SQL

DBMSs offer various ways to interact with databases, including Graphical User Interfaces (GUIs) and Structured Query Language (SQL). GUIs provide a user-friendly way to manage databases, while SQL is a standardized language used for querying and manipulating data.

Interacting via GUI

Most major DBMSs come with graphical management tools that enable users to perform data operations without writing SQL code. Some common GUI tools include:

1. **MySQL Workbench**: A visual tool for MySQL that allows users to design, develop, and administer MySQL databases.

2. **pgAdmin**: A powerful, open-source administration and development platform for PostgreSQL.

3. **Oracle SQL Developer**: A free integrated development environment that simplifies the development and management of Oracle databases.

4. **SQL Server Management Studio (SSMS)**: An integrated environment for managing any SQL infrastructure, from SQL Server to Azure SQL Database.

5. **MongoDB Compass**: A graphical user interface for MongoDB which allows users to query, visualize, and analyze data easily.

Using these tools, users can create and manage database schemas, perform data entry, execute queries, and monitor database performance through visual dashboards.

Interacting via SQL

SQL is a versatile and powerful language that allows for detailed data manipulation and retrieval. Each DBMS implements its own version of SQL, although the core syntax remains largely the same across platforms.

Common SQL Operations

1. **Create Table**: Define a new table in the database.

```sql
CREATE TABLE students (
    id INT PRIMARY KEY,
    name VARCHAR(100),
    age INT
);
```

2. **Insert Data**: Add records into a table.

```sql
INSERT INTO students (id, name, age)
VALUES (1, 'John Doe', 20);
```

3. **Select Data**: Retrieve records from a table.

```sql
SELECT * FROM students;
```

4. **Update Data**: Modify existing records in a table.

```sql
UPDATE students SET age = 21 WHERE id = 1;
```

5. **Delete Data**: Remove records from a table.

```sql
DELETE FROM students WHERE id = 1;
```

6. **Join Tables**: Combine records from two or more tables based on related columns.

```sql
SELECT students.name, courses.course_name

FROM students

JOIN course_enrollments ON students.id = course_enrollments.student_id

JOIN courses ON course_enrollments.course_id = courses.id;
```

SQL provides powerful querying capabilities,

including aggregate functions, filtering, sorting, and complex joins, enabling users to manage and analyze data effectively.

In conclusion, Chapter 2 explores the essential concepts surrounding Database Management Systems, along with an overview of leading DBMS platforms like MySQL, PostgreSQL, Oracle, SQL Server, and MongoDB. Through careful installation and configuration, users can efficiently manage data, utilizing both GUI tools and SQL commands for effective data manipulation and retrieval. This foundational knowledge prepares database administrators and developers for effectively harnessing data in today's information-driven world.

Chapter 3: SQL Language

In the landscape of database management, Structured Query Language (SQL) emerges as a fundamental component for developers, database administrators, and data analysts. This chapter delves into the intricacies of SQL, covering its definition, basic commands, advanced functionalities, transaction management, and techniques for optimizing queries.

What is SQL?

Structured Query Language (SQL) is a standard programming language specifically designed for managing and manipulating relational databases. It is essential for creating, querying, updating, and deleting data stored within a relational database management system (RDBMS). SQL serves as a bridge between end-users and the complex underlying data storage, enabling individuals to interact with data without needing in-depth programming knowledge.

The foundation of SQL lies in its declarative nature, where users describe what they want to achieve rather than explicitly stating how to do it. This conceptual ease allows for efficient data management and retrieval. SQL is an ANSI (American National Standards Institute) standard, which ensures its wide adoption across numerous database systems, including MySQL, PostgreSQL, Oracle, SQL Server, and SQLite.

SQL consists of several components, including:

1. **Data Query Language (DQL)**: Used for querying information from the database (e.g., using the SELECT statement).

2. **Data Definition Language (DDL)**: Used for defining and managing database

structures (e.g., CREATE, ALTER, DROP commands).

3. **Data Manipulation Language (DML)**: Involved with manipulating and managing data (e.g., INSERT, UPDATE, DELETE commands).

4. **Data Control Language (DCL)**: Used for defining access control and permissions (e.g., GRANT, REVOKE commands).

This versatility makes SQL a powerful tool for database administration, establishing its necessity in various application domains.

Basic Commands

Understanding SQL starts with mastering the basic commands which form the backbone of data manipulation. The four primary commands in SQL are SELECT, INSERT, UPDATE, and DELETE, often referred to as CRUD operations (Create, Read, Update,

Delete).

1. SELECT

The SELECT statement is used to query and retrieve data from a database. It allows users to specify exactly which columns of data they wish to see and from which tables. A basic SQL SELECT statement could look like:

```sql
SELECT column1, column2, columnN
FROM table_name
WHERE condition;
```

For example, to retrieve names and email addresses from a `users` table where the country is 'USA':

```sql
SELECT name, email
FROM users
WHERE country = 'USA';
```

2. INSERT

The INSERT statement is used to add new records to a table. The syntax for inserting data is straightforward:

```sql
INSERT INTO table_name (column1, column2, columnN)
VALUES (value1, value2, valueN);
```

For example, to add a new user to the `users` table:

```sql
INSERT INTO users (name, email, country)
VALUES ('John Doe', 'john@example.com', 'USA');
```

3. UPDATE

The UPDATE statement is used to modify existing records in a table. It is crucial to use the WHERE clause to specify which records should be updated; without it, all records in the table would be affected:

```sql
UPDATE table_name
```

SET column1 = value1, column2 = value2

WHERE condition;

```
```

For instance, to change the email address of a specific user:

```sql
UPDATE users

SET email = 'john.doe@example.com'

WHERE name = 'John Doe';
```

4. DELETE

The DELETE statement is employed to remove records from a table. Similar to UPDATE, it is essential to use a WHERE clause to avoid unintentional data loss:

```sql
DELETE FROM table_name
WHERE condition;
```

To delete a user from the `users` table:

```sql
DELETE FROM users
WHERE name = 'John Doe';
```

These basic commands furnish users with the fundamental tools necessary to interact with SQL databases. However, SQL's true power emerges with more complex features, such as advanced functions and subqueries.

Advanced Functions and Subqueries

In addition to basic commands, SQL provides advanced functions and subqueries that enhance data handling capabilities.

Advanced Functions

SQL offers a variety of built-in functions to perform calculations on data. Common categories include:

- **Aggregate Functions**: Such as COUNT(), SUM(), AVG(), MIN(), and MAX(), aggregate functions summarize data over a set.

  For instance, to count the total number of users in the database:

```sql
SELECT COUNT(*) FROM users;
```

- **String Functions**: Functions like CONCAT(), LENGTH(), and UPPER() manipulate string data, providing formatting and transformation options.

Example of concatenating two strings:

```sql
SELECT CONCAT(first_name, ' ', last_name) AS full_name
FROM users;
```

- **Date Functions**: Functions like NOW(), DATEADD(), and DATEDIFF() facilitate date and time manipulation, essential for temporal data analysis.

To find records created in the last 30 days:

```sql
SELECT * FROM users
WHERE created_at >= NOW() - INTERVAL 30 DAY;
```

Subqueries

Subqueries, or nested queries, allow you to perform a query within another SQL query. This powerful feature enhances SQL's flexibility by enabling users to work with dynamic data sets.

A subquery can exist in several clauses, such as SELECT, WHERE, and FROM:

```sql
SELECT column1
FROM table_name
WHERE column2 IN (SELECT column2 FROM another_table WHERE condition);
```

For example, to select users who have made purchases, assuming there's a `purchases` table with a `user_id`:

```sql
SELECT name
FROM users
WHERE id IN (SELECT user_id FROM purchases);
```

Subqueries can significantly simplify complex queries and are often essential in structuring efficient and effective SQL statements.

Transaction Management

In environments with multiple users and concurrent data access, transaction management becomes paramount. SQL transactions ensure data integrity and consistency, even in cases of failure or concurrent updates.

A transaction is a sequence of one or more SQL operations that are executed as a single unit. SQL uses specific commands to manage transactions:

- **BEGIN TRANSACTION**: Initiates a new transaction.

- **COMMIT**: Applies all changes made

during the transaction.

- **ROLLBACK**: Reverses all changes made during the transaction if an error occurs.

For example, consider a scenario where you need to transfer funds between two accounts in a banking system:

```sql
BEGIN TRANSACTION;

UPDATE accounts

SET balance = balance - 100

WHERE account_id = 'A123';

UPDATE accounts

SET balance = balance + 100

WHERE account_id = 'B456';
```

```
COMMIT;
```

If any step in this transaction fails (for example, if the account 'A123' does not have sufficient funds), executing a ROLLBACK ensures that no changes are made, maintaining data integrity:

```sql
ROLLBACK;
```

Implementing robust transaction management is crucial for ensuring data reliability and consistency, especially in critical systems where data accuracy is non-negotiable.

Query Optimization

As databases grow in size and complexity, the efficiency of SQL queries becomes paramount. Optimizing queries ensures that results are retrieved quickly and resources are utilized effectively.

Indexing

One of the primary techniques for query optimization involves indexing. An index is a database object that improves the speed of data retrieval operations on a table, acting like a roadmap to find data without scanning the entire table.

Creating an index on a specific column can significantly improve the query performance:

```sql
CREATE INDEX idx_email ON users(email);
```

Query Structure

Crafting well-structured queries can also enhance performance. This involves:

- Selecting only the necessary columns instead of using `SELECT *`.

- Applying appropriate WHERE clauses to limit result sets.

- Avoiding complex joins when simpler subqueries will suffice.

Analyzing Execution Plans

Database management systems often provide tools to analyze query execution plans. An execution plan breaks down how SQL processes a query step by step, allowing users to identify bottlenecks and optimize performance.

By utilizing `EXPLAIN` in front of a SELECT statement, users can gain insights into how the database engine interprets the query:

```sql
EXPLAIN SELECT name FROM users WHERE country = 'USA';
```

Understanding execution plans helps users refine their SQL statements, resulting in faster query performance.

Caching

Implementing caching mechanisms can reduce database load and improve application response times. Frequently accessed data can be stored in a cache, eliminating the need for repetitive database queries.

By combining these techniques, database administrators and developers can create a robust framework for both writing and optimizing SQL queries, ensuring they perform well under various conditions.

SQL serves as the backbone of database management, enabling users to interact with sophisticated data structures easily. By understanding its basic commands, exploring advanced functionalities and subqueries, mastering transaction management, and implementing optimization techniques, individuals can wield the power of SQL to manage and manipulate data effectively.

As data continues to grow exponentially in our digital landscape, mastering SQL becomes increasingly crucial, forming an essential skill for anyone involved in data management and analysis. SQL not only allows for efficient data handling but also empowers organizations to make informed decisions based on accurate and timely information. Prioritizing continuous learning and adaptation to SQL's evolving features will ensure lasting relevance in the ever-changing field of data management.

Chapter 4: Database Security

Database security is a critical aspect of data management. In an era where data breaches and cyber threats are increasingly common, database administrators (DBAs) must implement robust security measures to protect sensitive information. This chapter delves into the fundamental principles of data security, access control, permissions, data encryption, and the essential practices of backup and recovery.

Principles of Data Security

The security of data within a database is guided by several foundational principles. These principles help create a framework that ensures data remains safe from unauthorized access, breaches, and other forms of compromise.

1. Confidentiality

Confidentiality ensures that sensitive data is only accessible to authorized individuals. This involves implementing various strategies to protect data from unauthorized access. Encryption of data at rest and in transit is one of the primary methods used to preserve confidentiality. By converting data into a format that is unreadable without an encryption key, organizations can mitigate the risks associated with data breaches.

2. Integrity

Integrity refers to the accuracy and consistency of data throughout its lifecycle. DBAs must ensure that data cannot be altered or deleted by unauthorized users. This is often achieved through the implementation of access controls and validation checks. For example, using checksums and hash functions can help verify that data has not been tampered with.

3. Availability

Availability ensures that authorized users have access to the data whenever they need it. This principle addresses potential threats that could render data inaccessible, such as system failures, attacks, or natural disasters. Implementing redundancy through backup systems, load balancing, and disaster recovery plans is essential to maintaining data availability.

4. Accountability

Accountability involves tracking who accessed and modified data, allowing organizations to maintain a clear audit trail. This is crucial for identifying potential breaches and understanding the actions taken by users. Implementing logging and monitoring tools can help DBAs maintain accountability and respond quickly to unauthorized access attempts.

5. Authenticity

Authenticity is the assurance that the data is genuine and sourced from reliable origins. To maintain authenticity, organizations should authenticate users before granting access to the database. This is commonly achieved through the use of various authentication methods, including passwords, tokens, and biometric verification.

Access Control and Permissions

Access control is a fundamental component of database security. It determines who can access the database and what operations they can perform. Effective access control mechanisms are essential to protect sensitive data from unauthorized access.

1. Role-Based Access Control (RBAC)

RBAC is a widely used access control method that assigns permissions based on user roles within an organization. Users are grouped into roles that align with their job responsibilities, and permissions are assigned to these roles rather than individual users. This simplifies the management of access rights and ensures that users only have access to the data necessary for their roles.

2. Principle of Least Privilege

The principle of least privilege dictates that users should only be granted the minimum level of access necessary to perform their job functions. This reduces the risk of accidental or malicious data exposure. DBAs should regularly review user access permissions to ensure compliance with this principle.

3. User Authentication

User authentication is crucial to confirming the identity of individuals attempting to access the database. A combination of strong passwords, two-factor authentication (2FA), and single sign-on (SSO) solutions can enhance authentication processes. DBAs should enforce policies that require users to choose complex passwords and change them regularly.

4. Access Control Lists (ACLs)

Access control lists are policies associating specific permissions with various users or groups for certain database objects. ACLs provide granular control over who can access and modify data, allowing for tailored permissions based on specific needs while maintaining security compliance.

5. Auditing and Monitoring

Auditing and monitoring access to the database is essential for identifying potential security breaches and ensuring compliance with regulations. By maintaining logs of database access and changes, DBAs can track who accessed what data and when, enabling them to investigate suspicious activities.

Data Encryption

Data encryption is one of the most effective methods to protect sensitive information within a database. It involves converting plain text data into a coded format, rendering it unreadable without the appropriate decryption key. Encryption is crucial for safeguarding data both at rest and in transit.

1. Encryption at Rest

Encryption at rest protects data stored within the database and servers. This may include encrypting entire database files or specific table columns that contain sensitive information. Techniques such as Transparent Data Encryption (TDE) can be utilized to encrypt data at rest without requiring changes to the application layer.

2. Encryption in Transit

Encryption in transit protects data as it travels between the database and user applications. Protocols such as Secure Sockets Layer (SSL) and Transport Layer Security (TLS) should be implemented to encrypt data transmitted over networks, safeguarding it from interception during communication.

3. Key Management

Effective key management is essential for maintaining data security. Organizations must implement robust policies for generating, storing, and rotating encryption keys. Compromised keys can lead to unauthorized access, so a secure key management system is vital to mitigate such risks.

4. Compliance and Standards

Many industries are governed by regulations that mandate the use of encryption to protect sensitive data. For example, organizations handling financial or healthcare information must comply with regulations such as the Payment Card Industry Data Security Standard (PCI DSS) and the Health Insurance Portability and Accountability Act (HIPAA). Understanding and adhering to applicable compliance standards is crucial for organizations handling sensitive data.

Backup and Recovery

Data backup and recovery are critical components of a comprehensive database security strategy. Ensuring the availability of data in the event of a breach, data corruption, or system failure is paramount for organizations.

1. Regular Backups

Regular database backups are essential for safeguarding data against unexpected disasters. Organizations should implement an automated backup schedule to ensure that data is backed up consistently. Backups should be stored securely, preferably in multiple locations (both on-site and off-site), to protect against data loss.

2. Incremental and Full Backups

A combination of full and incremental backups can optimize storage and recovery time. A full backup captures the entire database, while incremental backups only capture changes made since the last backup. This strategy reduces the time and storage required for backups and expedites the recovery process.

3. Testing Backup Restores

It's not enough to create backups; organizations must regularly test the restoration process to ensure that data can be efficiently recovered. Conducting periodic recovery drills helps verify the integrity of backups and reinforces the effectiveness of recovery procedures.

4. Disaster Recovery Planning

A well-defined disaster recovery plan is crucial for ensuring business continuity. DBAs must develop strategies for recovering data after a breach or data loss incident. This plan should include predefined protocols for assessing damage, restoring backups, and communicating with stakeholders.

5. Documentation and Compliance

Maintaining documentation of backup and recovery procedures is vital for regulatory compliance and internal governance. Organizations should have clear policies outlining backup schedules, storage locations, and recovery procedures, ensuring accountability and standardization.

Conclusion

Database security is an ongoing challenge that requires a multifaceted approach that spans principles of data security, access control, encryption, and backup and recovery strategies. DBAs play a crucial role in safeguarding sensitive data and ensuring compliance with regulatory standards. By understanding and implementing best practices in these areas, organizations can significantly reduce their risk of data breaches and maintain the integrity and confidentiality of their databases.

In a landscape where cyber threats are ever-evolving, continuous monitoring, regular updates to security policies, and education for staff on security awareness will further strengthen database security, providing a resilient framework that can adapt to emerging security challenges. Implementing these strategies effectively enables organizations to harness the value of their data while protecting against potential risks.

Chapter 5: Database Maintenance and Monitoring

In the realm of database management, ensuring the integrity, availability, and performance of data systems is crucial. As database administrators (DBAs), we assume the responsibility of maintaining these systems through various practices aimed at ensuring that they function optimally, even as demands and technologies evolve. This chapter delves into the essential tasks associated with the maintenance and monitoring of databases, including routine maintenance activities, performance monitoring, troubleshooting common issues, and backup planning.

Routine Maintenance Activities

Routine maintenance activities are vital to ensure that the database operates efficiently and effectively. These activities include:

1. Regular Updates and Patching

Ensuring that the database management system (DBMS) and any other related software are updated is paramount. Regular updates and patches protect databases from vulnerabilities and ensure compatibility with new technologies. Most DBMS vendors regularly release patches that not only fix security vulnerabilities but also improve performance and introduce new features. DBAs must stay abreast of these updates and apply them in a timely manner.

2. Performance Tuning

Performance tuning is an ongoing task that involves analyzing the database to improve its efficiency. This can involve re-evaluating indexing strategies, optimizing queries, and adjusting configuration settings based on usage patterns. DBAs often use performance monitoring tools to gather data on query performance, locking issues, and resource utilization to identify bottlenecks.

3. Index Maintenance

Indexes significantly improve the speed of data retrieval operations. However, over time, indexes can become fragmented, which adversely affects performance. Routine index maintenance tasks involve:

- **Rebuilding Indexes:** This process reorganizes the physical storage of the index to improve performance.

- **Defragmenting Indexes:** This keeps the indexes efficient by minimizing fragmentation.

- **Updating Statistics:** Statistics inform the query optimizer about data distribution, helping it to create efficient execution plans.

4. Data Purging and Archiving

As databases grow, it's important to manage the volume of data to ensure optimal performance. Regular data purging and archiving involve removing obsolete data that is no longer needed or moving it to less expensive storage solutions. This practice helps maintain data relevance while optimizing performance.

5. Health Checks

A proactive approach to database health includes performing regular health checks. These checks can involve:

- Verifying disk space availability.

- Monitoring CPU and memory usage.

- Checking for long-running or blocking queries.

- Reviewing logs for any anomalies or warnings.

Performance Monitoring

Effective performance monitoring is crucial for anticipating problems before they affect the database operation and ensuring the overall efficiency of the data management system.

1. Monitoring Tools

Numerous tools assist DBAs in monitoring database performance. These can range from built-in tools provided by the DBMS to third-party applications that offer advanced analytics. Essential metrics to monitor include:

- **CPU Usage:** High CPU usage may indicate poorly optimized queries or an insufficiently sized database server.

- **Memory Usage:** Databases can consume significant memory, especially with larger datasets, and inadequate memory can lead to performance issues.

- **Disk I/O:** Monitoring disk read/write times can help identify bottlenecks. Slow disk responses can severely impact database performance.

2. Key Performance Indicators (KPIs)

DBAs should employ KPIs to evaluate the performance of the database system systematically. Common KPIs include:

- **Query Response Time:** The amount of time it takes to execute a query.

- **Throughput:** The number of transactions processed within a specific time frame.

- **Wait Times:** Amounts of time spent waiting for resources (e.g., locks, IO) can help identify performance bottlenecks.

3. Query Analysis

Query performance is pivotal to overall database efficiency. DBAs should regularly analyze slow queries and utilize query execution plans to gain insights into how queries are executed by the database engine.

Understanding the execution plans can lead to adjustments that significantly improve performance.

4. Alerting Mechanisms

Setting up alerting mechanisms is vital for proactive monitoring. Alerts can notify DBAs of critical thresholds being exceeded (e.g., CPU usage above 90%). Establishing these alerts allows for rapid response to potential performance issues before they escalate into more serious problems.

Troubleshooting Common Issues

Despite meticulous upkeep and monitoring, issues can still arise within database systems. Understanding common problems and their resolutions is key for DBAs.

1. Slow Performance

A common symptom within database management is slow performance. DBAs should start by:

- Monitoring currently executing queries to identify long-running ones.

- Reviewing resource usage to identify potential bottlenecks in memory, CPU, or disk I/O.

- Analyzing execution plans for poorly performing queries to identify a need for indexing or optimization.

2. Deadlocks

Deadlocks occur when two or multiple transactions are waiting for each other to release locks. To resolve a deadlock situation:

- Review application logic to minimize lock contention.

- Apply timeout settings to automatically retry transactions if they are waiting for too long.

- Use deadlock detection features provided by

many modern DBMS.

3. Connectivity Issues

Connectivity problems can stem from network issues, server configuration errors, or resource constraints. Troubleshooting involves checking network connections, server logs, and configuration settings. Ensuring that proper firewall rules and permissions are in place is critical for maintaining connectivity.

4. Data Corruption

Data corruption can occur due to hardware failures, software bugs, or improper shutdowns. Regularly checking logs and using checksums can help identify corruption early. In more severe cases, restoring data from backups may be necessary.

5. Version Compatibility

Changes in software versions, such as

upgrading the DBMS, can lead to compatibility issues with applications or extensions. It is essential to test upgrades in a staging environment before rolling them out in production to identify and resolve potential problems.

Backup Planning

Backup planning is a cornerstone of database maintenance, ensuring that data is not only preserved but can also be restored effectively.

1. Types of Backups

Understanding the different types of backups is essential for effective backup planning:

- **Full Backups:** These create a complete copy of the database. They serve as baseline backups and may be performed weekly or bi-weekly.

- **Incremental Backups:** These only back

up the data that has changed since the last backup (full or incremental). They are less time-consuming and help save storage space.

- **Differential Backups:** These back up all changes made since the last full backup. They are larger than incremental backups but can be easier to restore.

2. Backup Schedule

Creating a backup schedule is essential for minimizing data loss. DBAs should assess the frequency needed based on how often data changes. Critical databases may require hourly incremental backups coupled with daily full backups, while less critical databases may have less frequent backups.

3. Testing Backups

Regularly testing backups is essential to ensure data can be restored when needed. Backups should not only be made but also verified to ensure their integrity and usability.

This involves:

- Regularly restoring backups to a staging environment to ensure they are functional.

- Conducting restore drills to ensure that staff members know how to restore operations in the event of an incident.

4. Secure Storage

Backups must be stored securely to prevent unauthorized access. Employing encryption is critical when storing backups, especially for sensitive data. Moreover, using off-site storage or cloud solutions can help protect against physical disasters that could impact local storage.

5. Documentation

Documenting backup procedures, schedules, and restoration processes is crucial for effective management. Clear documentation supports consistency in operations and assists team members in executing backup and restoration procedures when necessary.

Maintaining and monitoring a database is an ongoing endeavor that requires vigilance, strategy, and execution. Through routine maintenance, effective performance monitoring, troubleshooting common issues, and meticulous backup planning, database administrators can ensure that data remains accessible, secure, and performant. As technology continues to evolve, so too will the practices and tools available to DBAs, making continual learning and adaptation essential components of effective database management.

Chapter 6: Data Design and Data Modeling

In this chapter, we will explore the critical aspects of database administration concerning data design and modeling. Our discussion will cover requirements analysis, the logical and physical design of databases, the creation of Entity-Relationship (ER) diagrams, and the testing of the data model. Each of these components plays a crucial role in ensuring that the database will effectively meet the needs of users and applications.

Requirements Analysis

Understanding User Needs

The first step in database design begins with requirements analysis. This involves engaging stakeholders, such as end users, business analysts, and project managers, to gather and document their needs. Understanding the specific requirements helps in developing a database that is both functional and efficient.

Techniques for conducting requirements analysis can include:

- **Interviews**: One-on-one discussions with stakeholders to extract detailed requirements.

- **Surveys and Questionnaires**: Collecting information from a larger audience to identify common requirements and expectations.

- **Workshops**: Collaborative sessions that bring together users to identify requirements through discussions and brainstorming.

- **Observation**: Directly viewing how current systems are used to identify gaps and opportunities for improvement.

Documenting Requirements

Once the requirements are gathered, they must be documented clearly and in detail. Effective documentation includes:

- **Functional Requirements**: What the system should do, including specific functionalities.

- **Non-functional Requirements**: Criteria such as performance, security, and usability that the system must meet.

- **Constraints and Assumptions**: Any limitations or assumptions made during the analysis phase that could impact the design process.

Use Cases and User Stories

Another important aspect of requirements analysis is the creation of use cases and user stories. Use cases detail the interactions between users and the system while user stories provide a more simplified version focusing on the needs and goals of users. Both tools provide valuable insights into the desired features of the database and the interactions that users will have with it.

Logical and Physical Design of the Database

Logical Design

Logical design involves translating the requirements identified during the analysis into a logical structure that lays out the organization of the data. This phase focuses on what data should be stored, their relationships, and the constraints on the data.

Data Normalization

A critical step in logical design is data normalization, where data is organized to reduce redundancy and improve data integrity. Normalization involves decomposing a database into smaller tables and defining relationships among them. The primary normal forms include:

- **First Normal Form (1NF)**: Ensures that the table has a primary key and that all attributes contain atomic values.

- **Second Normal Form (2NF)**: Addresses partial dependency; all non-key attributes must depend on the entire primary key.

- **Third Normal Form (3NF)**: Eliminates transitive dependencies; non-key attributes must be directly dependent on the primary key.

Entity-Relationship (ER) Model

The next step in logical design typically involves creating an Entity-Relationship model. An ER model visually represents the data entities, their attributes, and the relationships among them. Entities are objects or concepts with stored data, while attributes are the data we want to collect about those entities.

Physical Design

Once the logical design is established, the next step is physical design, which focuses on the actual implementation in the database management system (DBMS). This includes:

- **Choosing a Suitable DBMS**: Assessing the requirements and selecting an appropriate DBMS such as MySQL, PostgreSQL, Oracle, or Microsoft SQL Server.

- **Defining Table Structures**: Translating the logical model into physical tables, specifying data types for each attribute, indexing strategies, and constraints (like primary keys, foreign keys).

- **Setting Up Relationships**:
Implementing the relationships established in the ER model through foreign keys and defining referential integrity constraints.

Performance Considerations

Physical design also must take into account performance factors such as indexing, partitioning, and the normalization/denormalization balance:

- **Indexing**: Creating indexes on frequently queried columns can drastically improve query performance.

- **Partitioning**: Dividing large tables into smaller, manageable pieces can improve performance and maintenance.

- **Denormalization**: In cases where performance is critical, some level of denormalization may be beneficial to reduce the complexity of queries.

ER Diagrams (Entity-Relationship Diagrams)

Definition and Purpose

ER diagrams are a pivotal tool in data modeling, providing a visual representation of the database structure. They highlight how entities relate to each other, making it easier for stakeholders to understand the design.

Components of ER Diagrams

ER diagrams consist of various components:

- **Entities**: Represented as rectangles, they signify objects or subjects in the database (e.g., Customer, Order).

- **Attributes**: Ellipses connected to

entities that describe characteristics (e.g., CustomerName, OrderDate).

- **Relationships**: Diamonds depict how entities interact with each other (e.g., A Customer places an Order).

- **Cardinality**: Indicated by symbols to show the nature of the relationship (one-to-one, one-to-many, many-to-many).

Creating ER Diagrams

Creating ER diagrams involves several steps:

1. **Identify Entities**: Based on requirements, identify the main entities that will be part of the database.

2. **Determine Attributes**: Specify the key attributes for each entity, ensuring that they align with user needs.

3. **Establish Relationships**: Define how entities will interact and detail the nature of

these relationships.

4. **Refine the Diagram**: Iterate on the diagram based on stakeholder feedback, ensuring it meets all requirements.

Tools for Designing ER Diagrams

There are many tools available for designing ER diagrams, including:

- **Lucidchart**

- **Microsoft Visio**

- **Draw.io**

- **ERDPlus**

These tools often provide templates and features that can aid in efficiently creating clear and professional diagrams.

Testing the Data Model

Importance of Testing

Testing the data model is a critical phase that ensures the structure aligns with requirements and functions as intended. An effective testing strategy involves several key components:

- **Validation of the Data Model**: Assessing that the ER diagram and the tables accurately represent the requirements.

- **Functional Testing**: Verifying that all required functionality works as expected.

- **Performance Testing**: Ensuring that the database performs adequately under expected loads.

- **Usability Testing**: Gathering feedback from users to assess whether the database meets their needs.

Approaches to Testing

1. **Unit Testing**: Testing individual components or functions of the database separately.

2. **Integration Testing**: Ensuring that components work together as expected.

3. **System Testing**: Verifying the complete database system's compliance with the specified requirements.

4. **User Acceptance Testing (UAT)**: Involving end users to validate that the database meets real-world needs and expectations.

Tools for Testing

Several tools can assist in database testing, including:

- **SQL Fiddle**: A platform for testing SQL queries and structures.

- **Postman**: Useful for testing API interactions with the database.

- **DBT (Data Build Tool)**: Helps manage database transformations and assertions.

- **Load Testing Tools**: Such as JMeter or Gatling to simulate user load and test performance.

Iterative Improvement

Through the testing process, it is essential to gather feedback and adapt the data model as necessary. This iterative approach allows database administrators to refine the design and ensure that it remains aligned with evolving business needs.

Conclusion

In conclusion, the phases of requirements analysis, logical and physical design, ER diagram creation, and testing form the foundation of successful database administration. Each component is interconnected, contributing significantly to the overall effectiveness and efficiency of the database system. As databases continue to evolve with advancing technologies and increasing user expectations, understanding these principles becomes increasingly important for database professionals. By adhering to these best practices, database administrators can design databases that not only meet current requirements but are also flexible enough to accommodate future growth and changes.

Chapter 7: Performance Optimization

In the realm of database management, performance optimization is a paramount activity that ensures that the database system operates efficiently and can handle the increasing demands of data processing. It involves a series of techniques and best practices aimed at improving the speed and efficiency of database operations. As data volume increases and the complexity of queries grows, database administrators (DBAs) find themselves tasked with ensuring that their systems can keep pace without degradation of service.

The significance of performance optimization lies not just in making systems faster but also in ensuring that they can scale effectively. Optimizing performance can lead to reduced resource consumption, which correlates with lower operational costs. Moreover, a well-optimized database enhances user experience by decreasing response times for applications reliant on that database.

This chapter delves into several key aspects of performance optimization: indexing and query tuning, resource management, and scalability and distribution of databases. Each of these components plays a critical role in ensuring that databases run seamlessly and can meet the demands of modern applications.

Indexing and Query Tuning

The Role of Indexes

Indexes are data structures that improve the speed of data retrieval operations on a database table at the cost of additional space. They are similar to the index in a book, allowing the database engine to quickly locate the relevant data without scanning every row in a table. There are various types of indexes, including single-column indexes, composite indexes, unique indexes, and full-text indexes. Understanding when and how to implement these indexes is crucial for performance optimization.

1. **Single-column Indexes**: These are created on a single column of a table. They are useful when queries frequently filter or sort by that column.

2. **Composite Indexes**: These involve multiple columns and are particularly valuable for queries that filter on multiple columns. The order of the columns in the index is significant and can impact performance.

3. **Unique Indexes**: These ensure that all values in the indexed column are distinct. They provide both uniqueness and indexing benefits.

4. **Full-text Indexes**: Used for searching text within string columns, full-text indexes

are essential for optimizing searches on large text fields.

Query Tuning Techniques

Query tuning involves rewriting or adjusting queries to improve performance. DBAs and developers can often find significant performance gains through careful analysis and modification of SQL statements. Here are some techniques:

1. **Use of Appropriate Joins**: The choice of join method (INNER JOIN, LEFT JOIN, RIGHT JOIN, etc.) can significantly impact query performance. Understanding the dataset and choosing the most efficient join type is crucial.

2. **Subqueries vs. Joins**: While subqueries can simplify complex queries, they can also lead to performance degradation if not used

judiciously. In many cases, rewriting subqueries as joins may yield better performance.

3. **Select Only Required Columns**: It's essential to avoid using SELECT * in queries. Instead, specify only the columns needed for the operation. This reduces the amount of data transferred and processed.

4. **Use WHERE Clauses**: Filtering data early in the query using WHERE clauses can significantly reduce the number of rows processed, leading to improved performance.

5. **Limit Result Sets**: When performing queries that are expected to return large result sets, it's beneficial to use LIMIT or equivalent clauses to restrict the number of records returned.

6. **Analysis of Execution Plans**: Most database systems provide tools to analyze how

a query is executed. Understanding the execution plan can reveal bottlenecks, such as full table scans or inefficient joins, allowing for targeted adjustments.

Regular Maintenance

Maintaining database performance is not a one-time task but an ongoing process. Regularly analyzing query performance, monitoring index usage, and performing routine maintenance activities like updating statistics and rebuilding indexes can help keep the database running optimally.

Resource Management

Efficient Use of Hardware Resources

Effective resource management involves ensuring that hardware resources like CPU, memory, and disk I/O are used efficiently.

Understanding the workload of your database —whether it is read-heavy, write-heavy, or balanced—can significantly impact configuration decisions.

1. **CPU Optimization**: Allocating enough CPU resources is vital, especially for compute-intensive operations. DBAs must monitor CPU usage and assess whether queries are consuming disproportionate amounts of CPU time.

2. **Memory Management**: Databases utilize memory for caching frequently accessed data. Proper configuration of memory allocation can lead to better performance. For example, setting an appropriate buffer cache size can result in reduced disk I/O.

3. **Disk I/O Considerations**: The speed of disk writing and reading operations can bottleneck database performance. Utilizing

faster storage solutions, such as SSDs, and ensuring that databases are properly partitioned can improve disk I/O performance.

Monitoring and Tuning Resource Consumption

Monitoring tools provide insights into database performance metrics, enabling DBAs to make informed decisions about where performance improvements can be made. Key metrics to watch include:

- Query execution time

- Index usage percentage

- Cache hit ratios

- Disk I/O statistics

- Active connections

Clusters of performance issues often reside in

under-tuned resources. For example, if the database runs many complex queries but the memory and CPU are insufficient to handle peak loads, performance will suffer. Regular performance reviews and benchmarks can highlight inconsistencies and areas needing adjustments.

Scalability and Distribution of Databases

Understanding Scalability

Scalability is the ability of a database to grow and manage increased loads without sacrificing performance. This can be achieved through vertical scaling (adding more power to existing resources) or horizontal scaling (adding more servers to handle the load).

1. **Vertical Scaling**: This approach involves upgrading the existing database server with more powerful hardware—more CPU cores, faster memory, etc. While

effective up to a point, vertical scaling has its limits.

2. **Horizontal Scaling**: This involves distributing the database load across multiple servers, often referred to as sharding. Sharding divides the dataset and places subsets on different servers. This increases throughput and availability.

Replication and High Availability

To enhance scalability and ensure continuous availability, database replication strategies can be employed. Replication involves copying data from one database server (the primary) to one or more other database servers (the replicas). Key strategies include:

- **Master-Slave Replication**: In this setup, one primary database handles all write operations while replicas can handle read queries. This offloads some of the read pressure from the primary database.

- **Multi-Master Replication**: This allows multiple databases to accept write operations, syncing data across them. While this offers higher availability, it comes with the complexity of conflict resolution.

Distributed Databases

In distributed database systems, data is spread across several physical locations. This architecture allows for greater fault tolerance, improved access speeds for geographically dispersed users, and better resource allocation.

Using distributed databases requires consideration of challenges such as network latency, data consistency, and partitioning strategies. Achieving the balance between data availability and consistency—often referred to as the CAP theorem—is a significant aspect of designing distributed database systems.

Final Thoughts on Performance Optimization

Performance optimization is an ongoing endeavor for database administrators. By implementing effective indexing strategies, tuning queries, managing resources wisely, and planning for scalability, DBAs can ensure their databases are not only performant today but also prepared for future growth. With the right tools, techniques, and strategies, maintaining high-performance databases becomes not just achievable but a fundamental aspect of effective data management.

As technology continues to advance, the methods and strategies for performance optimization will evolve. Staying informed about the latest developments, best practices, and tools in the field will be essential for any aspiring or current database administrator committed to excellence in database performance management.

Chapter 8: Working in Teams and Agile

In the rapidly evolving landscape of database management, the role of a Database Administrator (DBA) extends far beyond mere data management. Collaboration, adaptability, and flexibility are critical as database systems play an integral part across various organizational areas. This chapter explores how DBAs can work effectively in team environments, leveraging Agile methodologies and DevOps practices to enhance productivity and innovation. We will also delve into the importance of strong documentation and communication skills in fostering efficient collaboration among distinct teams, such as development, IT, and support.

Collaboration with Other Departments

Importance of Cross-Departmental Collaboration

In any organization, data lies at the heart of strategic decision-making. As such, DBAs must work closely with several departments, including development teams that build applications, IT teams responsible for infrastructure, and support teams that assist end-users. Effective collaboration ensures that database designs are not only efficient and scalable but also align with the needs of other departments.

1. **Development Teams**: DBAs collaborate with developers to ensure that the database design supports application requirements. This partnership helps in designing normalized database schemas that enhance data integrity and minimize redundancy. Furthermore, developers often rely on DBAs for understanding data access patterns and defining the best approaches to query optimization.

2. **IT Teams**: With foundational IT infrastructure playing a crucial role in database performance and availability, DBAs work alongside IT professionals to monitor system health, manage backups, and ensure that databases are secured against unauthorized access. Collaboration with networking teams is essential for optimizing data flow and ensuring sufficient resources for database operations.

3. **Support Teams**: Support teams interact directly with end-users and, therefore, provide critical insights into how database issues affect functionality. DBAs must work with support staff to identify recurring issues and proactively implement solutions. The DBA can also play a role in training support teams about the database architecture to enable them to provide better assistance.

Activities That Foster Collaboration

To enhance collaboration with other departments, DBAs can engage in the following activities:

- **Participate in Daily Standups**: Many Agile teams conduct daily standups where team members share what they did yesterday, what they plan to do today, and any impediments to progress. By participating in these sessions, DBAs can stay informed about development timelines, impending changes, or new requirements that might impact database design.

- **Attend Joint Planning Sessions**: In a scrum framework, planning sessions are crucial for aligning goals and estimates. A DBA's input during these sessions ensures that database needs are factored into the scheduling and priority of development tasks.

- **Share Knowledge**: Organizing joint workshops or training sessions allows DBAs and other teams to share expertise. For instance, a DBA could conduct a session on efficient database access patterns, while developers could provide insights into the application's needs, creating a shared understanding.

Agile Methodologies and DevOps

The Agile Mindset for DBAs

Agile methodologies emphasize iterative development, flexibility, and customer collaboration. The Agile principles resonate well with database administration practices, especially in environments that require rapid iterations and responsiveness to changing requirements.

- **Responding to Change**: DBAs should embrace the Agile principle of responding to change over following a pre-set plan. When a new feature requires database schema modifications, rather than rigidly adhering to older designs, DBAs should quickly assess the new requirements and adapt accordingly.

- **Continuous Improvement**: By practicing continuous improvement, DBAs can refine processes related to performance tuning, backup and recovery strategies, and security measures regularly based on feedback and performance metrics.

Integration of DevOps Practices

DevOps is a combination of development and operations aimed at shortening the development life cycle while delivering high software quality. For DBAs, incorporating DevOps practices can lead to improved collaboration and efficiency.

1. **Automation**: Automation of routine

tasks such as database backups, updates, and monitoring can free up a DBA's time, allowing them to focus on more strategic tasks. Tools like Jenkins or Ansible can help automate deployment pipelines for database changes alongside application updates.

2. **Version Control**: Implementing version control systems for database schemas, similar to code, allows teams to manage changes effectively, track revisions, and roll back to previous states when needed. Tools like Liquibase or Flyway are specifically designed for database version control.

3. **Collaboration Tools**: Utilizing tools like Slack, Jira, or Microsoft Teams fosters real-time communication and collaboration between DBAs and other teams. These platforms allow for instant messaging, file sharing, and issue tracking, which streamlines problem resolution.

Effective Documentation and Communication

The Role of Documentation

Effective documentation serves as a critical bridge for communication among teams. In environments where rapid changes occur, documentation helps maintain clarity on database structures, processes, and best practices.

1. **Database Design Documentation**: Documenting the database schema, relationships, and constraints gives developers a clear understanding of how data is structured. This resource proves invaluable when onboarding new team members or troubleshooting issues.

2. **Change Logs**: Maintaining a comprehensive log of changes made to the

database, including schema updates and performance tuning efforts, offers transparency into the evolution of the database and aids in troubleshooting and audits.

3. **Standard Operating Procedures (SOPs)**: Creating SOPs for regular tasks such as backups, restores, and incident responses ensures that team members can handle operations efficiently and consistently, even in the absence of the DBA.

Communication Skills

Strong communication skills are essential for DBAs to convey complex information effectively to both technical and non-technical stakeholders.

1. **Active Listening**: By actively listening during meetings and discussions, DBAs can better understand the needs and concerns of

other departments. This practice also helps in fostering mutual respect and trust among team members.

2. **Clarity in Reporting**: DBAs often need to present technical findings to upper management or business stakeholders. Clarity, conciseness, and the ability to translate technical jargon into layman's terms are necessary for ensuring that important database decisions are backed by understanding among all parties involved.

3. **Feedback Loop**: Establishing a feedback loop with team members promotes an environment of openness and continuous improvement. Regular check-ins can help DBAs gather insights on how database performance affects application functionality, allowing for proactive measures.

Tools for Documenting and Communicating

Several tools can assist DBAs in managing documentation and enhancing communication:

- **Confluence**: An effective platform for team collaboration, where documentation can be created, shared, and discussed. This tool allows for organized projects and knowledge bases.

- **Trello**: A project management tool that can help track tasks, visualize workload, and enhance collaboration across teams through shared boards.

- **Google Docs**: Facilitates real-time collaboration and editing of documentation, which can be crucial for dynamic teams that require up-to-date information on rapidly changing projects.

Database administration in a collaborative environment is a multifaceted role that entails not only technical expertise but also strong interpersonal skills and adaptability. By working closely with developers, IT, and support teams, DBAs can foster a culture of collaboration and innovation. Embracing Agile methodologies and DevOps practices enhances responsiveness to change and fosters efficiency. Furthermore, effective documentation and communication are vital for maintaining transparency and minimizing misunderstandings. As organizations increasingly rely on data-driven decisions, the role of the DBA as a collaborative partner becomes ever more crucial to achieving overall business success. By honing these skills and practices, DBAs can contribute to an agile and seamless integration within their teams and the broader organizational framework.

Chapter 9: Certifications and Career Opportunities for Database Administrators

Overview of DBA Certifications

In the rapidly evolving field of information technology, certifications serve as an essential benchmark for skill validation and professional development. For Database Administrators (DBAs), certifications not only enhance expertise in database management systems but also open pathways for career advancement and increased earning potential. Various organizations offer industry-recognized certifications tailored to different database management systems, including Oracle, Microsoft SQL Server, MySQL, and PostgreSQL, among others.

Popular DBA Certifications

1. **Oracle Certified Professional (OCP)**:

Oracle's OCP is one of the most respected certifications, highlighting advanced skills in Oracle database management. This certification covers various aspects of database management, such as automation, backup, recovery, performance tuning, and security.

2. **Microsoft Certified: Azure Database Administrator Associate**:

As cloud services gain prominence, Microsoft's certification focuses on administering cloud-based databases using Azure. It validates skills in database security, monitoring performance, and implementing high availability.

3. **Certified MySQL Database Administrator**:

Offered by Oracle, this certification validates skills related to MySQL database setup, configuration, and administrative tasks. It covers essential topics such as security, backup, and recovery.

4. **AWS Certified Database – Specialty**:

This certification is intended for DBAs working with Amazon Web Services. It focuses on database design, migration, deployment, and management on the AWS platform.

5. **PostgreSQL Certified Professional**:

This certification validates an individual's skills and knowledge in managing PostgreSQL databases, covering installation, configuration, and maintenance.

Importance of Certifications

Certifications act as a positive signal to employers, showcasing commitment to professional growth and a thorough understanding of specific technologies. They can lead to higher salaries, job stability, and opportunities for advancement. Additionally, many organizations have specific certifications they prefer or even require for DBA roles, making them a valuable asset on any resume.

How to Prepare for a Certification

Preparing for a DBA certification requires a comprehensive approach, integrating formal training, hands-on experience, and self-study. Here are some steps to effectively prepare for certification exams:

1. Understand Certification Requirements

Each certification has specific prerequisites, including prior experience and foundational knowledge. Familiarize yourself with the certification objectives, topics covered, and format of the exam. Most certification bodies provide detailed syllabus information to guide your studies.

2. Enroll in Training Courses

Many training providers offer courses tailored to certification preparation, either in-person or online. These courses can provide structured learning and comprehensive coverage of needed topics. Consider also attending workshops, webinars, and boot camps centered around the specific technologies related to the certification.

3. Utilize Official Study Materials

Most certification organizations provide official study guides, practice tests, and resources. Investing in these materials can help reinforce your knowledge and ensure you are familiar with the exam format.

4. Hands-On Practice

Theory alone isn't enough; practical experience is crucial for passing most DBA certifications. Set up your own lab environment to practice database installation, configuration, and administration tasks. You can leverage cloud services for hands-on labs without significant upfront investment in hardware.

5. Join Study Groups and Forums

Engaging with peers can enhance your preparation experience. Study groups and online forums can help answer questions, share study resources, and provide motivational support. A community of like-minded professionals can also keep you accountable to your study goals.

6. Take Practice Exams

Taking practice exams can significantly improve your readiness. They help you familiarize yourself with the types of questions you might face, assess your knowledge gaps, and time yourself under exam-like conditions. Many certification websites and third-party providers offer practice tests at various price points.

7. Review, Revise, and Relax

In the final days before your exam, focus on reviewing key concepts and revising areas where you feel less confident. Make sure to get plenty of rest before the exam day—being well-rested will improve your focus and performance.

Career Opportunities and Professional Development

With the growing demand for data

professionals, DBAs enjoy a plethora of career opportunities across various industries, including finance, healthcare, technology, and education. The role of a DBA is fundamental in managing data, ensuring its availability, security, and integrity.

1. Career Progression Paths

A DBA's career can evolve into various roles as one gains experience and additional skills. Here are a few potential career paths:

- **Senior Database Administrator**: Senior DBAs handle more complex system architectures, guide junior staff, and lead projects that require advanced knowledge.

- **Database Architect**: This role typically involves designing and implementing database solutions, requiring an in-depth understanding of database systems and business requirements.

- **Data Analyst/Scientist**: Transitioning into a data-oriented role can leverage a DBA's knowledge of data management and utilization to analyze data and generate insights.

- **Data Engineer**: A bridge role that blends database management with data warehousing and processing, data Engineers construct systems that allow data to flow from various sources into databases effectively.

- **Database Manager**: In supervisory positions, DBAs can oversee teams of database professionals, providing strategic direction on data management policies and practices.

2. Continuing Education

To remain competitive and relevant in the job market, DBAs should commit to ongoing education and professional development. Many organizations value employees who keep their skills up-to-date with the latest technologies and methodologies.

- **Online Courses**: Websites like Coursera, edX, and LinkedIn Learning offer a variety of courses related to database technologies, cloud platforms, and data analytics.

- **Conferences and Workshops**: Attending industry conferences allows DBAs to network, learn from experts, and discover new trends in database technology.

- **Webinars and Virtual Meetups**: Many organizations conduct regular webinars on trending topics in database administration. These sessions can provide insights and techniques that improve daily practice.

3. Networking and Professional Associations

Being part of professional networks and associations can provide significant advantages. Organizations such as the International Institute of Business Analysis (IIBA) and the Data Management Association (DAMA) offer networking opportunities, conferences, and professional resources that can aid in career growth. Networking can lead to mentorship, job opportunities, and collaborations that enrich professional experience.

4. Specialty Areas

As a DBA, you may also find opportunities to specialize in specific areas such as database security, big data technologies, or cloud database services. Specializing can set you apart from others in the field, making you more attractive to employers.

5. The Future of DBA Roles

With the increased emphasis on data-driven decision-making, the role of the DBA is evolving. Emerging technologies, such as artificial intelligence (AI) and machine learning (ML), are becoming integral to database management. DBAs who embrace these technologies and adapt to the rapid transformations in data management practices will position themselves for long-term career success.

The landscape for Database Administrators continues to expand, presenting numerous certifications and career opportunities. By investing time in preparation, professional development, and networking, DBAs can significantly enhance their career prospects and contribute meaningfully to their organizations. As the reliance on data continues to grow, so too will the demand for skilled DBAs, making this a prime time to be in this profession. Embracing continuous learning and staying attuned to industry changes will equip DBAs to navigate their careers successfully in this dynamic field.

Chapter 10: Technical Terms and Glossary

In the field of database administration, there are numerous technical terms and concepts that professionals need to be familiar with in order to effectively manage, design, and troubleshoot database systems. This chapter serves as a comprehensive glossary that covers these essential terms, offering definitions, explanations, and examples to illustrate their significance in the domain of database management.

1. Database

A **database** is an organized collection of data that is stored and accessed electronically, typically through a database management system (DBMS). A database allows users to efficiently manage large amounts of information, facilitating easy data retrieval, manipulation, and the application of business rules.

Example: A library database that contains records of books, authors, and borrowers.

2. Database Management System (DBMS)

A **DBMS** is a software application that interacts with end users, applications, and the database itself to capture and analyze data. It provides tools for creating, retrieving, updating, and managing data, ensuring data integrity and security.

Example: MySQL, Oracle Database, Microsoft SQL Server, and PostgreSQL are popular DBMS options.

3. Relational Database

A **relational database** organizes data into

tables that can be linked—or related—based on data common to each. The tables are structured in a way that ensures data integrity and minimal redundancy.

Example: A customer database that includes separate tables for customers, orders, and order details, which can all be linked through a unique customer ID.

4. SQL (Structured Query Language)

SQL is the standard programming language used to manage and manipulate relational databases. It encompasses commands for querying data, updating records, and creating or modifying database structures.

Example: A sample SQL query to retrieve customer names from a database may look like:

```sql

SELECT name FROM customers WHERE
status = 'active';

```

5. Table

A **table** is a structured set of data
elements (values) that are organized in rows
and columns. Each table represents a different
entity, such as users or products, and consists
of attributes (columns) that define the
characteristics of that entity.

Example: A 'Products' table may have
columns for product ID, name, price, and
stock quantity.

6. Row

A **row**, also called a record or tuple, represents a single instance of data within a table. Each row contains values for each of the table's columns.

Example: In a 'Customers' table, a single row could represent a customer named John Doe with the following details: customer ID, name, email address, and phone number.

7. Column

A **column** is a vertical entity in a table that contains all the information associated with a specific attribute of the entity represented by the table. Each column has a defined data type.

Example: In a 'Users' table, columns might include: user ID (integer), username (string), email (string), and registration date (date).

8. Primary Key

A **primary key** is a unique identifier for a record in a database table. It ensures that each record can be uniquely identified, preventing duplication and maintaining data integrity.

Example: A 'Users' table may use `user_id` as the primary key to distinguish each user record from others.

9. Foreign Key

A **foreign key** is a column or group of columns in a table that matches the primary key column of another table. It creates a relationship between the two tables.

Example: In an 'Orders' table, the

`customer_id` column serves as a foreign key referencing the primary key `customer_id` in the 'Customers' table.

10. Index

An **index** is a database object that improves the speed of data retrieval operations on a table. An index creates a data structure that allows the DBMS to find rows more quickly.

Example: Creating an index on the `username` column of a 'Users' table may speed up searches for user accounts by username.

11. Normalization

Normalization is the process of organizing a database to reduce data redundancy and improve data integrity. It involves dividing large tables into smaller, related tables and defining relationships between them.

Example: Instead of having a single table that contains information about students, their courses, and instructors, normalization would involve creating distinct tables for students, courses, and instructors, linking them with relationships.

12. Denormalization

Denormalization is the process of combining tables to reduce the complexity of data operations and improve read performance, often at the cost of additional storage and potential redundancy.

Example: Merging student, course, and instructor tables into one comprehensive table may speed up data retrieval for reports but may introduce redundancy.

13. Transaction

A **transaction** is a sequence of one or more database operations that are executed as a single unit. Transactions ensure data integrity by adhering to the ACID properties (Atomicity, Consistency, Isolation, Durability).

Example: A financial transaction in which funds are transferred between two accounts consists of a debit from one account and a credit to another, both operations must succeed or fail together.

14. ACID Properties

The **ACID properties** are a set of principles that guarantee reliable processing of database transactions:

- **Atomicity**: Ensures that all operations within a transaction are completed successfully or none at all.

- **Consistency**: Guarantees that a transaction will bring the database from one valid state to another, maintaining all defined rules.

- **Isolation**: Ensures that transactions are executed in isolation from one another, preventing interference.

- **Durability**: Ensures that the results of a committed transaction are permanently recorded, even in the case of a system failure.

15. Data Integrity

Data integrity refers to the accuracy and consistency of data stored in a database. Ensuring data integrity involves setting up rules and constraints to prevent errors or invalid data entries.

Example: A database might restrict entry of negative values for stock quantities, enforcing integrity.

16. Backup and Restore

- **Backup** is the process of creating copies of database data to be stored securely, allowing recovery in case of data loss.

- **Restore** is the process of retrieving data from backup files to recover a database to a previous state.

Example: Regularly scheduled backups help ensure that a database can be restored in the event of accidental deletion or corruption.

17. Schema

A **schema** is the structure of a database including the tables, fields, relationships, and constraints that define how data is organized and accessed. It acts as a blueprint for the database design.

Example: A database schema for a university might include tables for students, courses, and enrollments, detailing their relationships.

18. Query

A **query** is a request for data or information from a database. Queries are typically written in SQL and can involve complex operations such as joins, filtering, and grouping.

Example: A query to find all students enrolled in a specific course might look like this:

```sql
SELECT students.name FROM students

JOIN enrollments ON students.id = enrollments.student_id

WHERE enrollments.course_id = 101;
```

19. Stored Procedure

A **stored procedure** is a precompiled set of SQL statements stored in the database that can be executed as a single call. Stored procedures help with code reusability and can improve performance.

Example: A stored procedure might handle user registration by inserting user data into the 'Users' table, ensuring that all necessary fields are correctly populated.

20. Trigger

A **trigger** is a set of instructions that are automatically executed in response to specific events on a particular table or view. Triggers are often used for enforcing business rules or maintaining audit trails.

Example: A trigger might automatically log every new entry in a 'Logins' table whenever a user successfully logs in to the system.

21. View

A **view** is a virtual table that is based on the result of a SQL query. Views do not store data themselves but provide a way to simplify complex queries, present data in a particular format, or restrict access to specific rows or columns.

Example: A view named 'ActiveUsers' might include only users with an active status, providing a simplified way to access essential user information.

22. Data Warehouse

A **data warehouse** is a centralized repository used for reporting and data analysis, often containing historical data collected from various sources. It is designed to facilitate queries and analysis, making it ideal for business intelligence.

Example: A company may use a data warehouse to aggregate sales data from multiple stores to analyze overall performance.

23. ETL (Extract, Transform, Load)

ETL refers to the process of extracting data from different sources, transforming it into a suitable format or structure for analysis, and loading it into a data warehouse or other target system.

Example: A retail company might use ETL processes to gather sales data from point-of-sale systems, clean and summarize it, and load it into a data warehouse for reporting.

24. NoSQL

NoSQL databases are a class of databases that provide a mechanism for storage and retrieval of data that does not require a fixed schema, often designed for high scalability and performance. Types of NoSQL databases include document stores, key-value stores, column-family stores, and graph databases.

Example: MongoDB is a widely used NoSQL database that stores data in a flexible, JSON-like format.

25. Cloud Database

A **cloud database** is a database service that runs on a cloud computing platform, offering scalability, flexibility, and remote access. Cloud databases can be either relational or NoSQL and are typically managed by a third-party service provider.

Example: Amazon RDS (Relational Database Service) allows users to set up, operate, and scale a cloud-based relational database.

26. Data Lake

A **data lake** is a centralized repository that stores structured and unstructured data at any scale. A data lake allows users to analyze large volumes of diverse data types without needing to predefine a schema.

Example: An organization might use a data lake for storing various data types, including log files, sensor data, images, and more, for later analysis.

27. Data Mining

Data mining is the process of discovering patterns and knowledge from large amounts of data using techniques from statistics, machine learning, and database systems. It is often used to extract valuable insights that can inform decision-making.

Example: Retailers may use data mining to analyze customer purchasing patterns to optimize inventory and marketing strategies.

28. Big Data

Big Data refers to extremely large datasets that may be analyzed computationally to reveal patterns, trends, and associations, especially relating to human behavior and interactions. Big Data challenges traditional data management and analysis techniques due to its volume, velocity, and variety.

Example: Social media platforms generate Big Data that can be mined for insights into user behavior and trends.

29. Data Governance

Data governance refers to the overall management of data availability, usability, integrity, and security within an organization. It includes establishing policies and standards for data management and ensuring compliance with regulations.

Example: A company may implement data governance practices to ensure that customer data is stored securely and used responsibly, adhering to regulations like GDPR.

30. Replication

Replication is the process of copying and maintaining database objects, such as tables, in multiple databases to ensure consistency and availability. It can be used for disaster recovery, load balancing, or ensuring high availability.

Example: A company may use database

replication to keep copies of its transactional database in multiple geographic locations for redundancy.

This glossary provides a foundation of essential technical terms that every database administrator should be familiar with. Mastery of these concepts not only enhances the ability to manage databases effectively but also enables professionals to communicate more effectively within the field, troubleshoot issues, and implement best practices in database management. Understanding the intricacies of database systems allows administrators to optimize performance, enhance security, and support the evolving data needs of organizations.

Index